Včera v noci jsem vzal Měsíc na procházku.
Plul za mnou jako klidný papírový drak,

Though there wasn't a string or a tail in sight
when I took the Moon for a walk.

Vzal jsem Měsíc na Procházku

I Took the Moon for a Walk

Written by Carolyn Curtis
Illustrated by Alison Jay

Czech translation by Vladislava Vydra

I took the Moon for a walk last night.
It followed behind like a still summer kite,

Přesto, že nebyl jeho ocásek ani struna v dohledu
když jsem vzal Měsíc na procházku.

I carried my blue torch just in case
the Moon got scared and hid its face.

Vzal jsem si jen pro případ sebou světlo
Měsíc se zalekl a schoval svou tvář.

Ale vykouknul z mraků jemných
jako krajka
Když jsem vzal Měsíc na procházku.

But it peeked through clouds
that were fragile as lace
When I took the Moon for a walk.

I warned the Moon to rise a bit higher
so it wouldn't get hooked on a church's tall spire,

Varoval jsem Měsíc aby se vyhoupl trochu výš
aby se nezachytil o štíhlou věž kostela,

While the neighbourhood dogs made a train-whistle choir when I took the Moon for a walk.

Zatím co psi v sousedství skučeli jako
pískající vlak
když jsem vzal Měsíc na procházku.

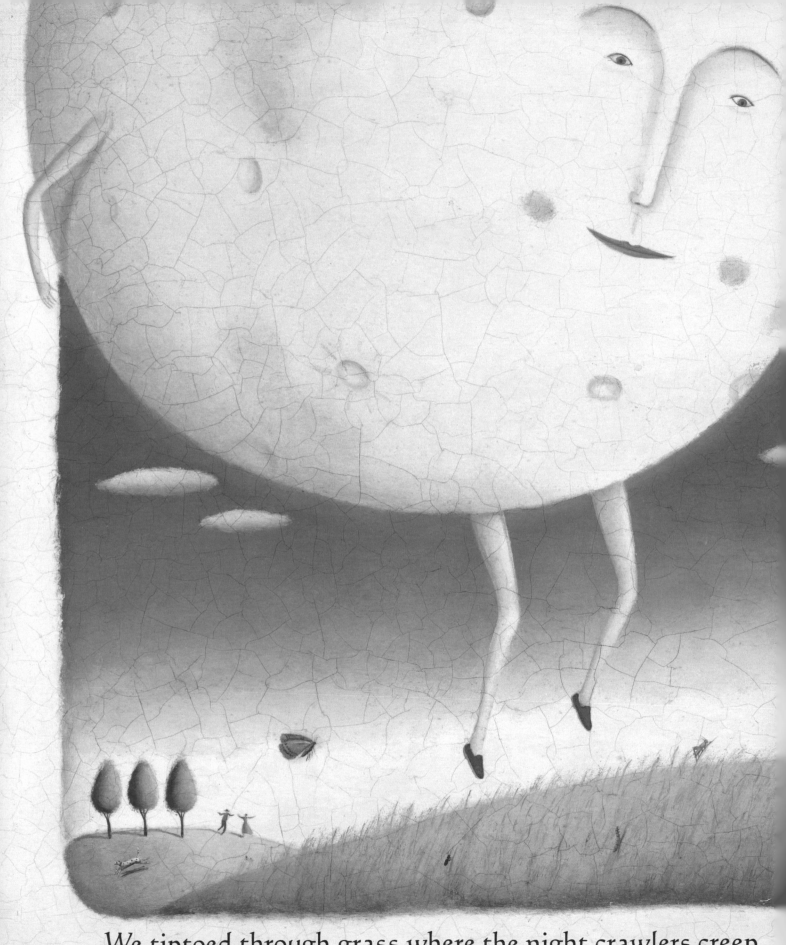

We tiptoed through grass where the night crawlers creep
when the rust-bellied robins have all gone to sleep,

Šli jsem po špičkách trávou kde se plíží hmyz
kde drozdi se svými zrzavě-červenými bříšky šli spát,

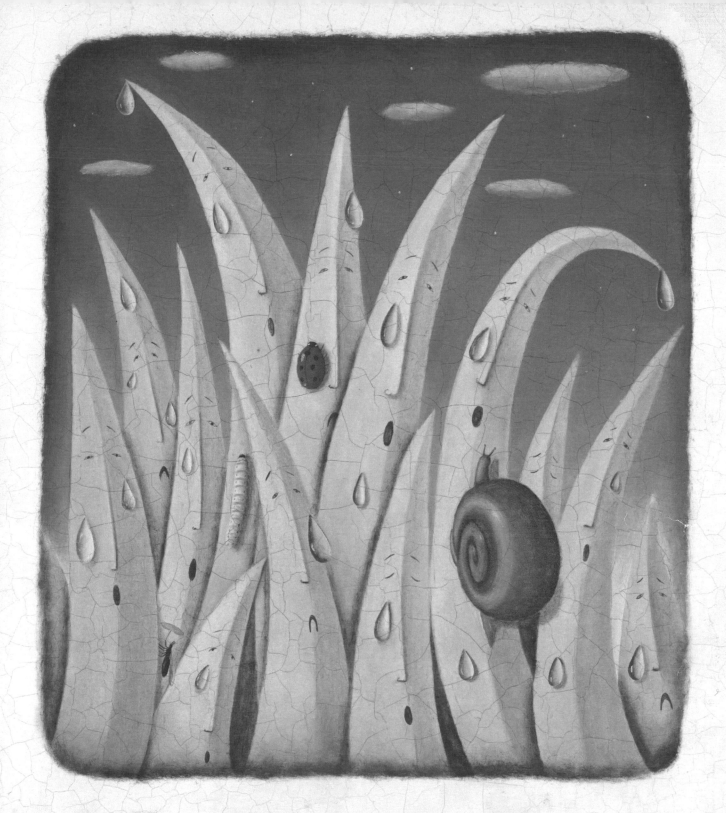

A Měsíc zavolal rosu aby spadla na trávu jako slzy
Když jsem vzal Měsíc na procházku.

And the Moon called the dew so the grass seemed to weep
When I took the Moon for a walk.

Houpali jsme se o závod a
vysoko jsem se odrazil
A představil si že mě Měsíc
požádal abych letěl s ním,

We raced for the swings,
where I kicked my feet high
And imagined the Moon had
just asked me to fly,

Hand holding hand through the starry night sky
when I took the Moon for a walk.

Držící se za ruce přes hvězdnatou noční oblohu
když jsem vzal Měsíc na procházku.

We danced 'cross the bridge where the smooth waters flow.
The Moon was above and the Moon was below,

Tancovali jsme přes mosty kde klidná voda plyne.
Měsíc se vyhoupl nad a sklouzl pod,

A ve světle mezi nimi jsem se v jeho
záři odrážel
Když jsem vzal Měsíc na procházku.

And bright in between them
I echoed in their glow
When I took the Moon for a walk.

Then as we turned back, the Moon kept me in sight.
It followed me home and stayed there all night,

Pak když jsme se vraceli, Měsíc mě na cestu svítil.
Plul za mnou až domů a zůstal tam celou noc,

And thanked me by sharing its sweet sleepy light
when I took the Moon for a walk.

A poděkoval mě tím, že se mnou
sdílel jeho příjemné uspávající světlo
když jsem vzal Měsíc na procházku.

The Mysterious Moon

What do you see when you look at the moon? Children who live in Europe and the United States imagine that they see a man when they look at the moon. Children in Japan and India see a rabbit, and children in Australia see a kitten. But all children, no matter where they live, look up in wonder at the same moon.

The moon is primarily made of rock with a small iron core. It creates no light of its own, but reflects sunlight.

The shape of the moon seems to change during the month because the sunlight strikes the moon at different angles as it travels through space. These shapes are called 'phases'. Here are some of the phases of the moon:

| *New Moon* | *Crescent Moon* | *Half Moon* | *Gibbous Moon* | *Full Moon* |

When the moon is growing larger in the sky, we say that it is 'waxing'. When it is growing smaller, we say that it is 'waning'.

For people all over the world, the moon has always been an important way to measure time. Although the solar calendar has become the standard international way of doing this, many people still use lunar, or moon, calendars.

The moon can be a friend to farmers and gardeners - those who follow tradition know that the best time to sow seeds and transplant young shoots is when the moon is waxing.

Moon festivals are celebrated in many societies. The Chinese Moon Festival is held during the Harvest Moon - the full moon that rises in mid-autumn.

Many Celtic and Native American festivals are also held at the time of the Harvest Moon, when the people give thanks for the harvest and for all living things on earth.

The World at Night

If you took the moon for a walk through your neighbourhood, what would you show it? What would you hear, and what would you see?

Wherever you are, you would probably see some nocturnal creatures - mammals, birds and insects that usually sleep during the day and come out at night. They are especially adapted to life under the moon and stars:

Cats have eyes that see very well in the dark.

Rabbits have large ears that capture sound across long distances.

Bats use sounds and echoes to help them fly safely and find food.

Fireflies light up at night so that they can find each other.

Owls have necks that can turn right around and huge, flat eyes that enable them to see other creatures that are far away.

Some flowers are nocturnal too. They bloom and release their fragrance after dark.

And although you are asleep during the night, your mind is not! During the day, your waking, or conscious, mind is active, but when you sleep, your dreaming, or unconscious, mind is busy. So, the world at night is not so quiet as it seems!

For my nephew Christopher, *who first walked with the moon*
and my mother Estella, *who held his hand*
For my father Harold, *the star we steer by*
and Lucan, *my sun*
and, of course, for Emilie, *for Everything* - C.C.

The author extends heartfelt thanks to the society of Children's Book Writers and Illustrators for generous support in the form of
a Barbara Karlin Grant, WarmLines Parent Resources, Jane Yolen, the Jeff Kelly and Newton Library Critique Groups, and Alison Keehn.

For Mark, happy moon walking, love from Alison.

Mantra Lingua TalkingPEN
Global House
303 Ballards Lane
London N12 8NP
www.mantralingua.com
www.talkingpen.co.uk